COPYRIGHT 2020 © DOUDOUSTUFF
ALL RIGHT RESERVED.
THE USE OF ANY PART OF THIS PUBLICATION REPRODUCED, TRANSMITTED IN ANY FORM OR BY ANY MEANS, ELECTRONIC, MECHANICAL, RECORDING OR OTHERWISE, OR RESTORED IN A RETRIEVAL SYSTEM, WITHOUT THE PRIOR CONSENT OF THE PUBLISHER IS AN INFRINGEMENT OF COPYRIGHT LAW.

I spy with my little eye something beginning with.......

A

I spied an
Acorn

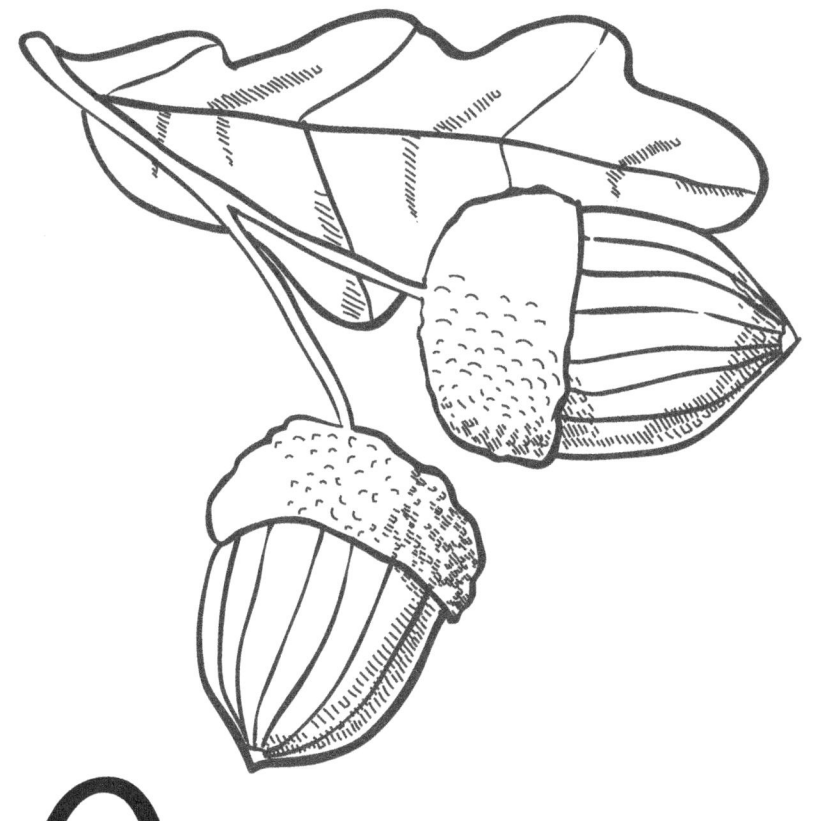

I spy with my little eye something beginning with.......

B

I spied

Bread

I spy with my little eye something beginning with.......

C

I spied a

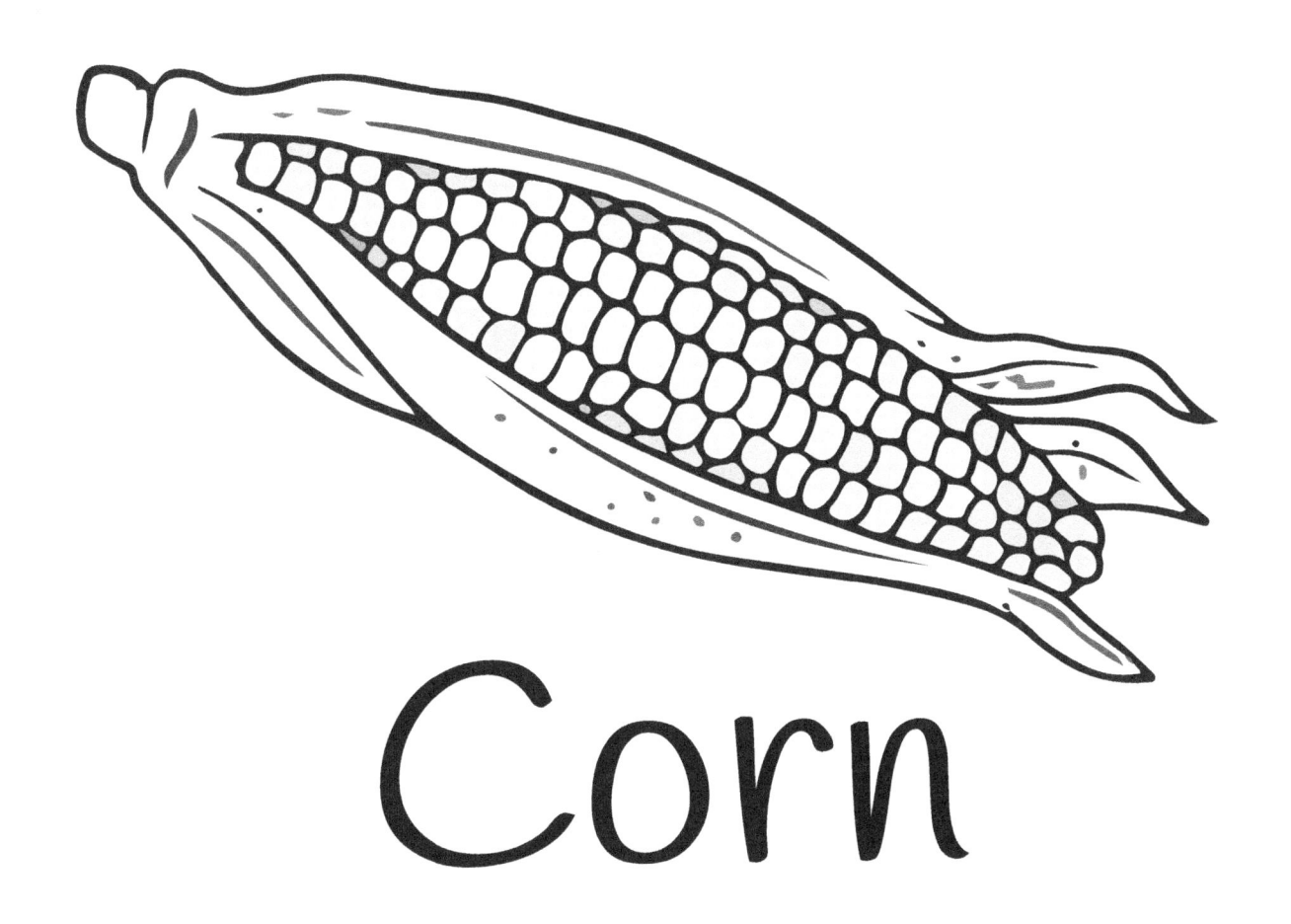

Corn

I spy with my little eye something beginning with.......

D

I spied a

Duck

I spy with my little eye something beginning with.......

E

I spied

Eggs

I spy with my little eye something beginning with....... F

I spied a

Fish

I spy with my little eye something beginning with....... G

I spied a

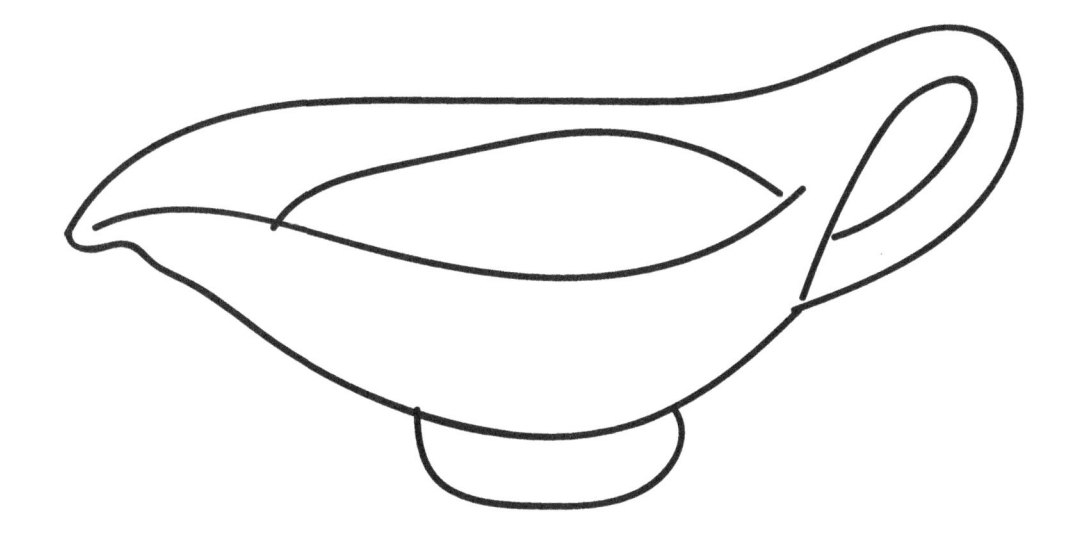

Gravy Boat

I spy with my little eye something beginning with.......

H

I spied a

Hat

I spy with my little eye something beginning with.......

I spied an

Ice Cream

I spy with my little eye something beginning with.......

J

I spied

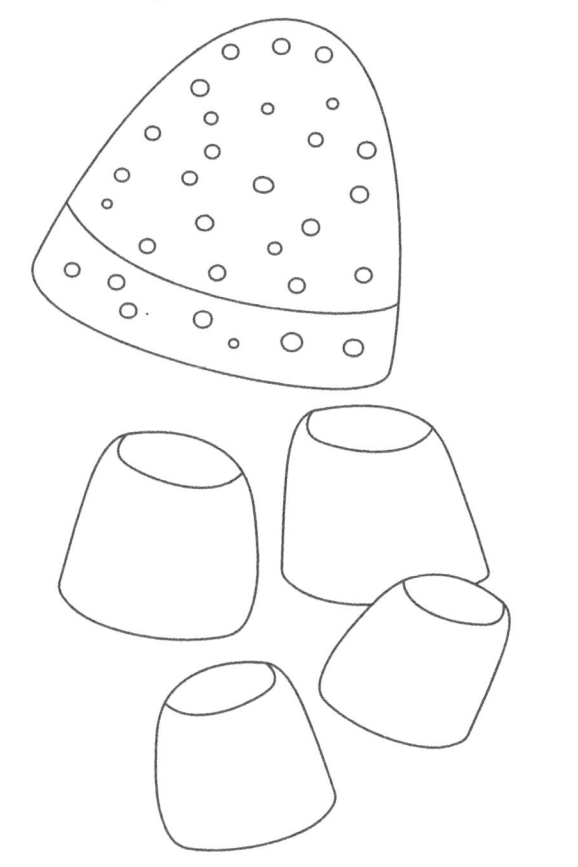

Jellies

I spy with my little eye something beginning with.......

K

I spied a

Kale

I spy with my little eye something beginning with.......

L

I spied a

Leaf

I spy with my little eye something beginning with.......

M

I spied a

Mayflower

I spy with my little eye something beginning with....... N

I spied a

Native American

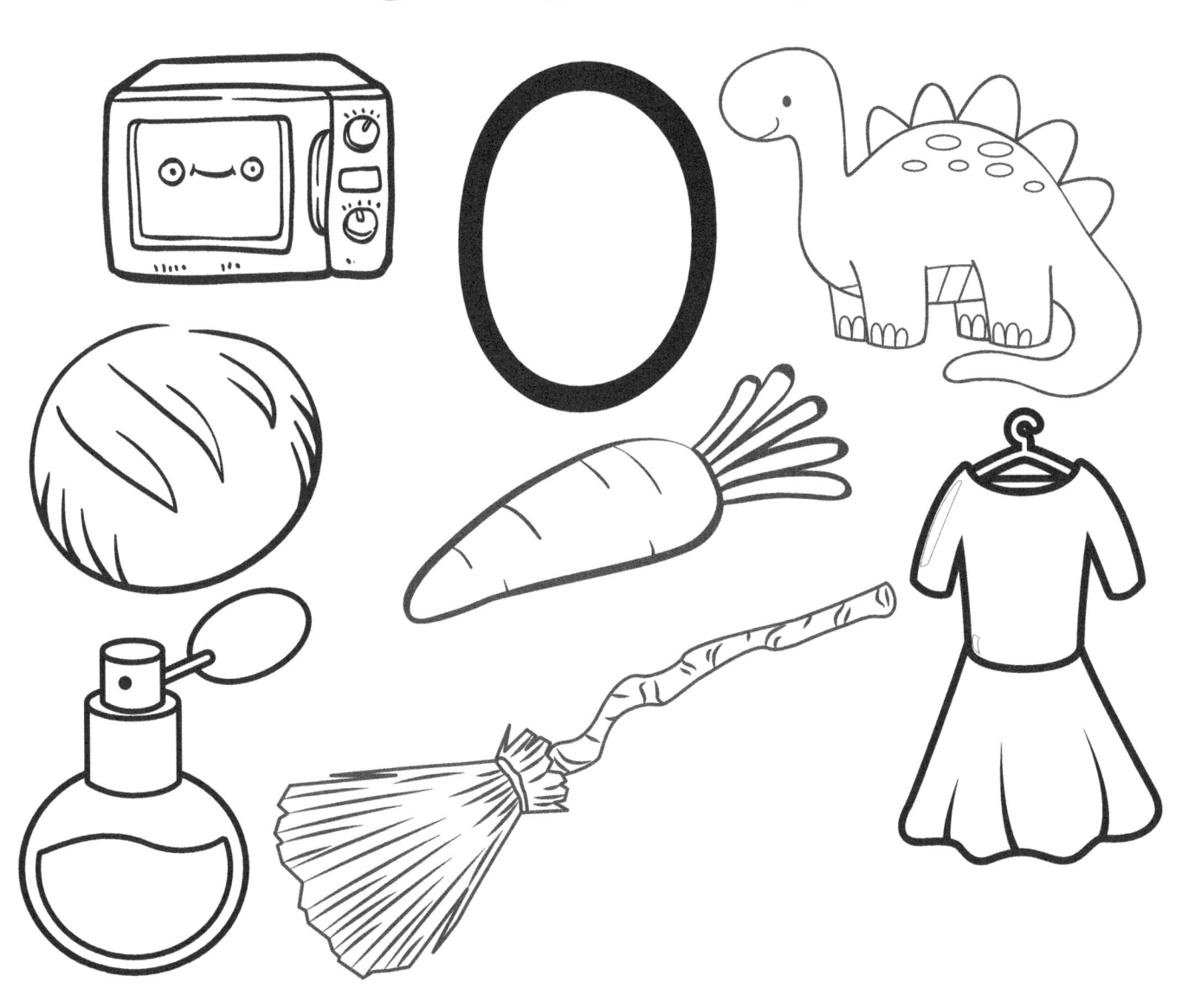

I spy with my little eye something beginning with.......

O

I spied an

Oven

I spy with my little eye something beginning with……

P

I spied a

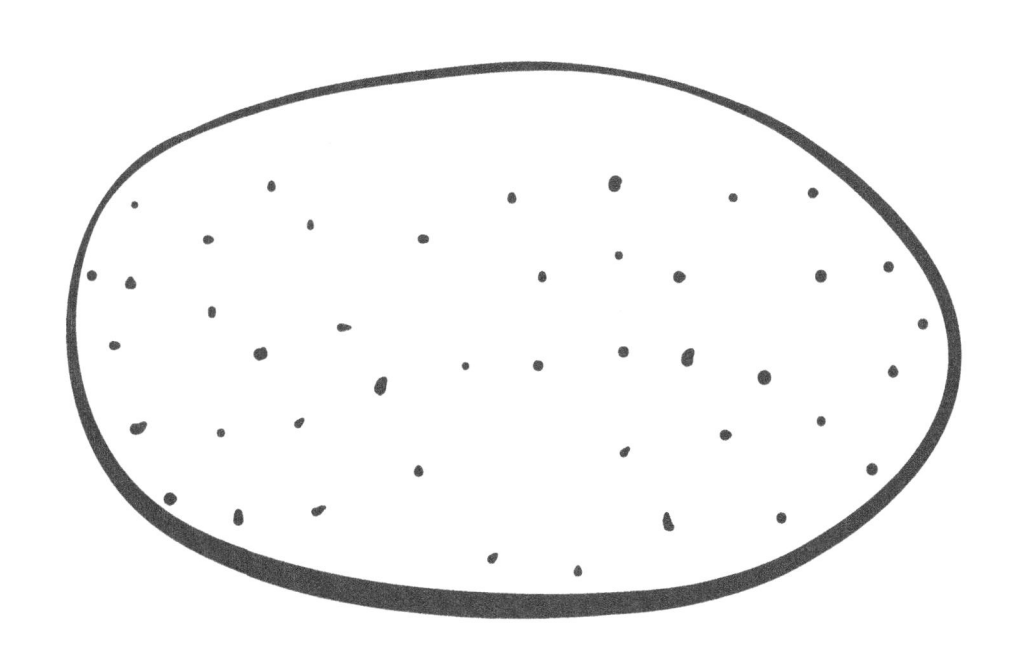

Potato

I spy with my little eye something beginning with.......

Q

I spied a

Quince

I spy with my little eye something beginning with.......

R

I spied a

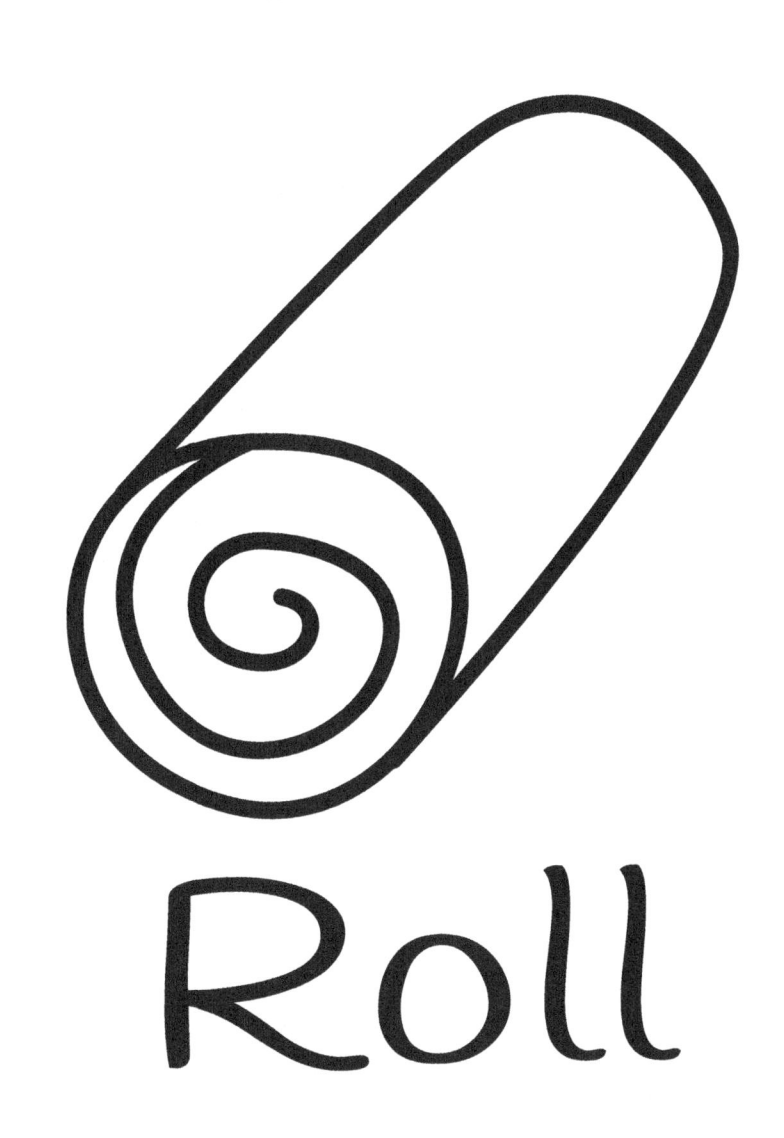

Roll

I spy with my little eye something beginning with.......

S

I spied a

Squirrel

I spy with my little eye something beginning with.......

T

I spied a

Turkey

I spy with my little eye something beginning with.......

U

I spied a

Uniform

I spy with my little eye something beginning with.......

V

I spied

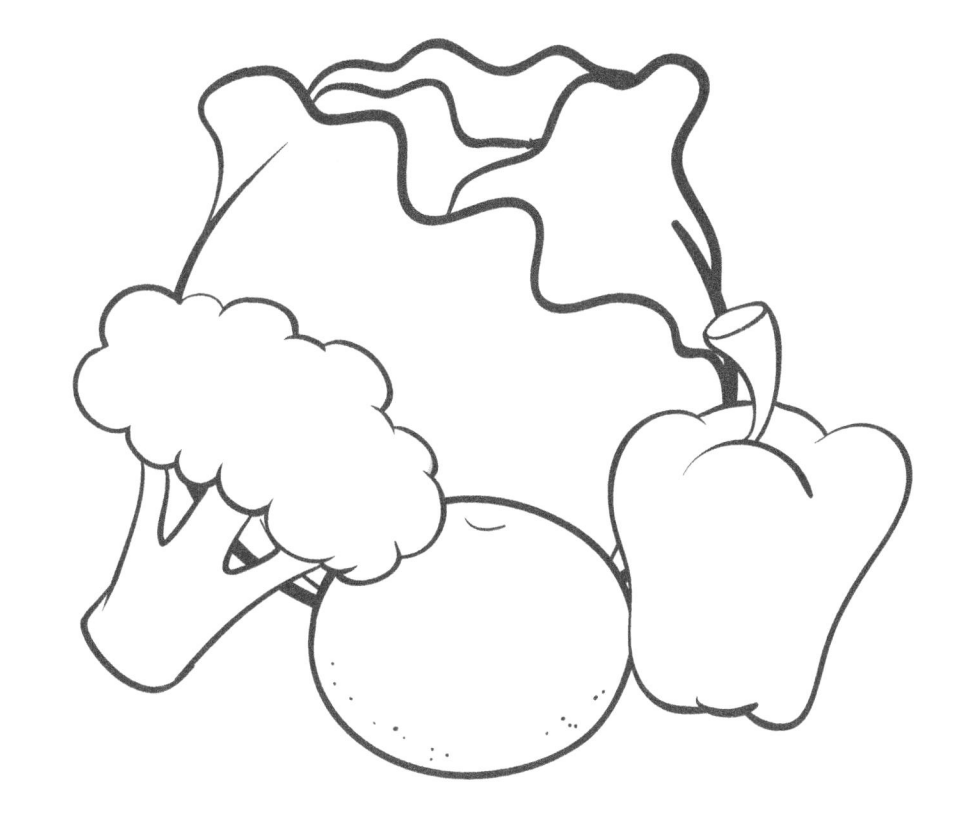

Vegetables

I spy with my little eye something beginning with.......

W

I spied a

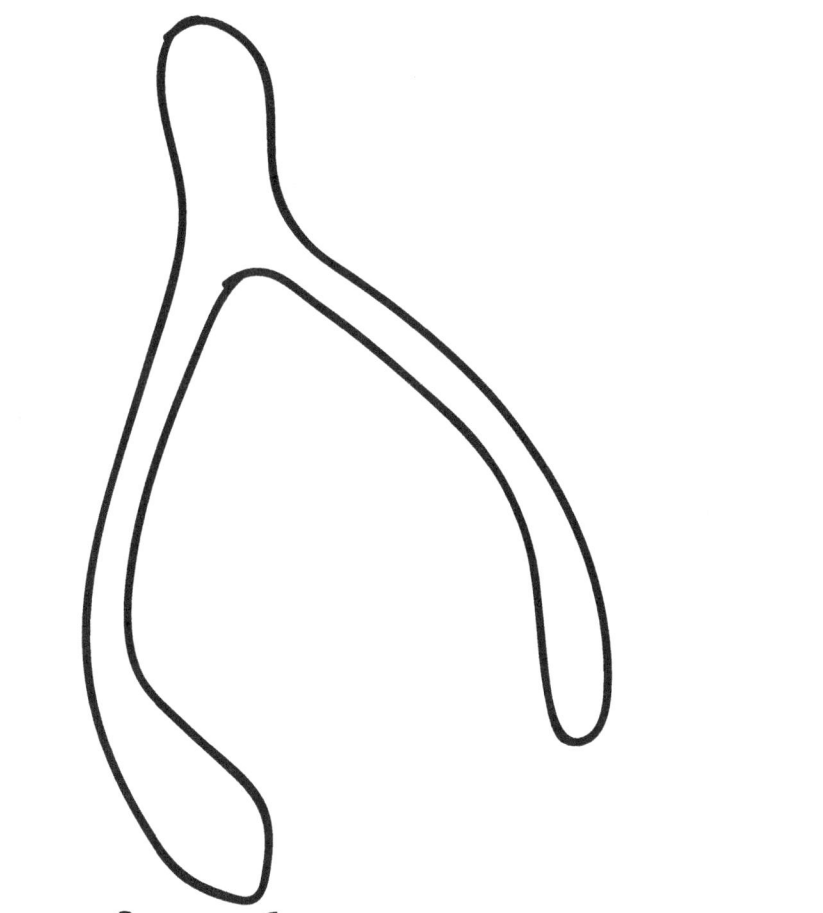

Wish Bone

I spy with my little eye something beginning with.......

X

I spied a

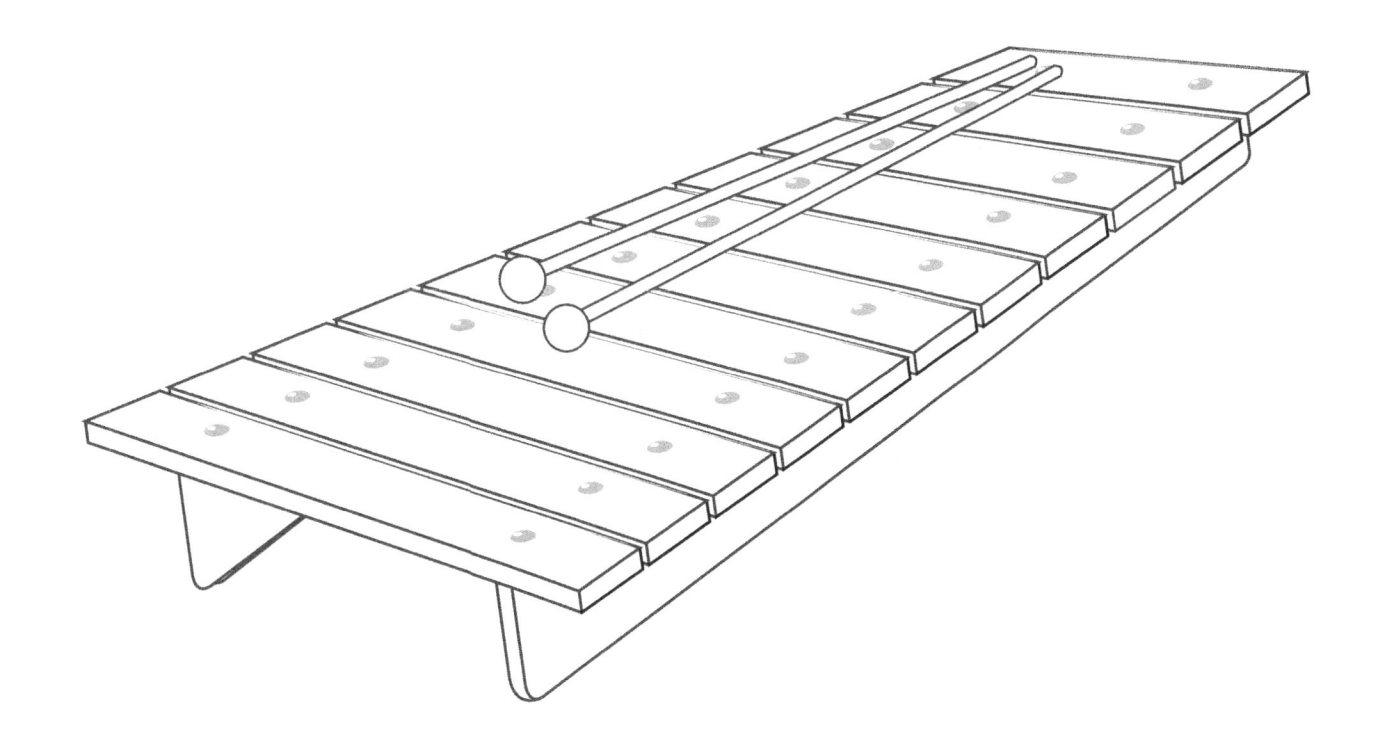

Xylophone

I spy with my little eye something beginning with.......

y

I spied a

Yam

I spy with my little eye something beginning with....... Z

I spied a

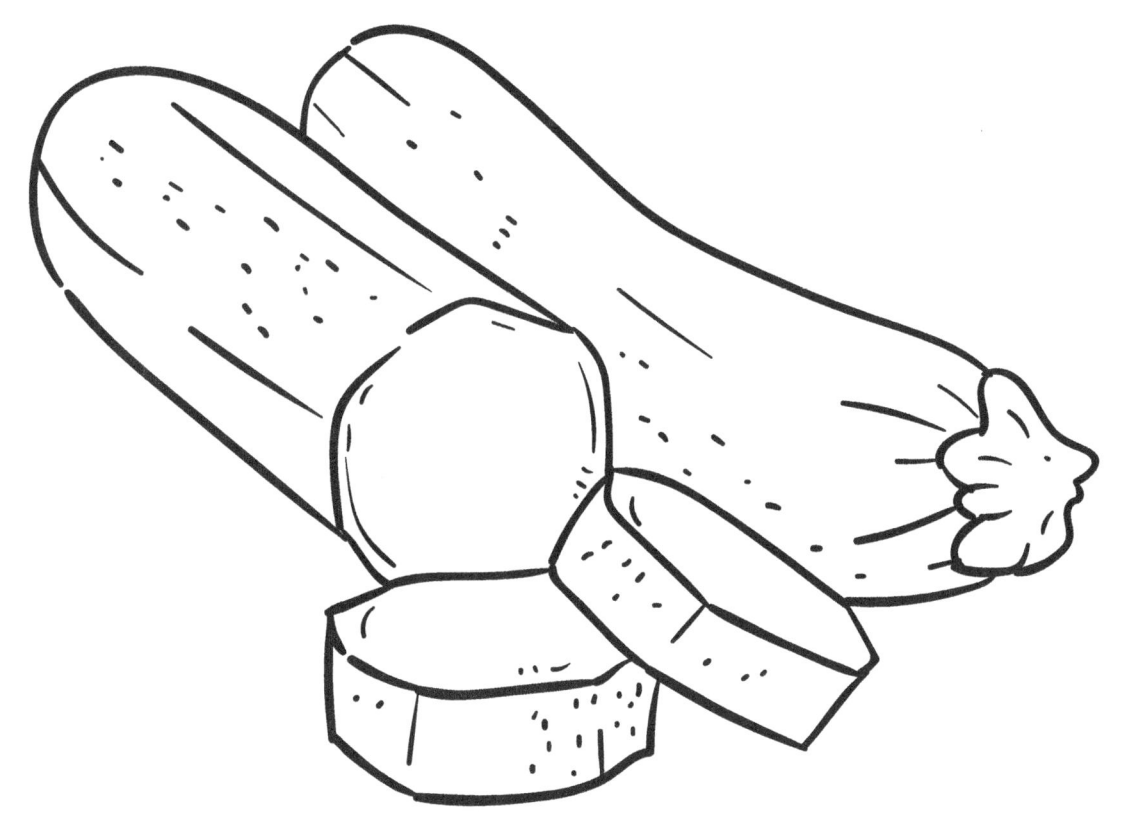

Zucchini

Made in the USA
Monee, IL
09 November 2022